ANIMALS IN OUR CARE
DOGS

Written by
Eliza Nodes

Genius Kid

American adaptation copyright © 2026 by North Star Editions, Mendota Heights, MN 55120. All rights reserved. No part of this book may be reproduced or utilized in any form or by any means without written permission from the publisher.

Dogs © 2024 BookLife Publishing
This edition is published by arrangement with BookLife Publishing

sales@northstareditions.com | 888-417-0195

Library of Congress Control Number:
2024952952

ISBN
978-1-952455-36-0 (library bound)
978-1-952455-92-6 (paperback)
978-1-952455-72-8 (epub)
978-1-952455-56-8 (hosted ebook)

Printed in the United States of America
Mankato, MN
092025

Written by:
Eliza Nodes

Edited by:
Elise Carraway

Designed by:
Ker Ker Lee

All facts, statistics, web addresses and URLs in this book were verified as valid and accurate at time of writing. No responsibility for any changes to external websites or references can be accepted by either the author or publisher.

Photo Credits – Images courtesy of Shutterstock.com, unless otherwise stated.

Cover – Eric Isselee, Studio13lights, MirasWonderland, Dorottya Mathe, TrapezaStudio, cynoclub, New Africa, ooodles, Iryna Kalamurza, Master1305, Anton Vierietin. 2–3 – zoyas2222, Eric Isselee. 4–5 –Nynke van Holten, Michaella Nielsen, photomaster. 6–7 – photomaster, Rosa Jay. 8–9 – kathrineva20, xkunclova, slowmotiongli, Julia Zavalishina. 10–11 – New Africa, Mega Vectors. 12–13 – Eric Isselee, Chase D'animulls, GPPets, TrapezaStudio, MirasWonderland, Jagodka, RTimages, E LLL, Nynke van Holten. 14–15 – FamVeld, alexei_tm. 16–17 – Eric Isselee, travelarium.ph, WilleeCole Photography. 18–19 – viktori__photo, Michar Peppenster, Mihail Pustovit, SasaStock, Brberrys. 20–21 – Eric Isselee, Svetlana Foote, J. Photos, cynoclub, Ingrid Pakats, domnitsky, smrm1977. 22–23 – lera lysenko, sophiecat, ANUCHA PONGPATIMETH, OlesyaPogosskaya, cynoclub.

CONTENTS

Page 4	Dogs
Page 6	The Canine Family
Page 8	Canine Faces
Page 10	Body of a Dog
Page 12	Breeds and Colors
Page 14	Caring for Your Dog
Page 16	Body Language
Page 18	From Puppy to Dog
Page 20	Believe It or Not!
Page 22	Are You a Genius Kid?
Page 24	Glossary and Index

Words that look like <u>this</u> can be found in the glossary on page 24.

DOGS

What do you think of when you hear a dog barking?

Dogs are known for being loyal and friendly.

Dogs come from wolves. They have a lot in common with their powerful <u>ancestors</u> and wild cousins.

All dogs and wolves are part of the Canidae <u>family</u>.
They are sometimes known as canines.

Dogs are mammals. This means they are warm-blooded, have a backbone, and make milk to feed their babies.

Dogs are omnivores. They eat plants and meat.

THE CANINE FAMILY

The canine family is split into 13 groups. These groups are based on how similar these canines are to each other.

Domestic dogs are in the same group as wolves. This group is called *Canis*.

DID YOU KNOW?

The scientific name for domestic dogs is *Canis lupus familiaris*.

African hunting dogs are in their own group called *Lycaon*.

Raccoon dogs are also in their own group. They are the only canines that <u>hibernate</u>.

Fennec foxes are the smallest canines.

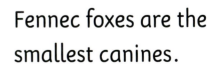

CANINE FACES

Let's look at the different parts that make up the face of a canine.

Dogs have around 18 muscles in each ear. They can move their ears in different directions to find sounds.

Dogs have strong eyesight at night. This is because their wolf ancestors hunted in the dark.

Smell is a dog's most powerful sense. Dogs use smell and sight to understand their surroundings.

Adult dogs have 42 teeth. Their teeth are sharp to cut through meat.

Dogs use their tongues to groom and clean their coats.

BODY OF A DOG

Dogs have around 320 bones in their body.

Dogs can only sweat from their paw pads and noses. So they keep their bodies cool by panting.

Some dogs have outer and inner coats. Their inner coats are short and keep them warm or cool. Outer coats have long, strong hairs to protect them against wet weather.

Dogs' tails help them balance and turn quickly when running.

Dogs use their strong claws for digging. This is useful for burying food and toys.

BREEDS AND COLORS

Poodle

Dogs come in many different <u>breeds</u>. Some dogs are purebred. Others are crossbreeds.

Purebreds are dogs whose parents are the same breed. There can be different colors within the breed.

Dachshund

Springer spaniel

DID YOU KNOW?
Labradors can be black, yellow, red, or chocolate.

Crossbreeds are dogs whose parents are different breeds. They can come in different colors.

Cockapoos are a cross between a cocker spaniel and a poodle.

Pomskies are a cross between a Pomeranian and a Siberian husky.

Chugs are a cross between a chihuahua and a pug.

CARING FOR YOUR DOG

Domestic dogs have some of the same natural <u>instincts</u> as wolves. Wolves hunt and chase for food. Dogs like to play by running and chasing. Playing fetch or catch is a good way for dogs to exercise. It encourages their natural instincts.

Wolves live in groups called packs. Packs care for and look after one another. Pet dogs see their human family as their pack. Spending lots of time with your dog will help to keep them happy.

DID YOU KNOW?
Around the world, more than 400 million dogs are kept as pets.

BODY LANGUAGE

Dogs can show how they are feeling with their bodies.

An angry dog might lean forward. Its ears might lie flat. It might show its teeth and possibly snarl or growl. This means it wants you to go away or stay away.

A worried dog might have its ears back and its tail tucked underneath its body. It may hold its paw in mid-air.

A happy dog will have its mouth open and wag its tail. If it wants to play, it may raise its bottom in the air and bark.

FROM PUPPY TO DOG

Baby dogs are called puppies. Puppies are born with their eyes closed. They find their mother by her smell and heat. For a few weeks, puppies mostly just sleep and drink their mother's milk. This gives them plenty of energy to grow.

When puppies are three or four weeks old, they can start being <u>weaned</u> off their mother's milk.

Dog

Puppy

Puppies become adults when they are one or two years old.

Female domestic dogs are pregnant for up to three months.

BELIEVE IT OR NOT!

All domestic dogs come from a type of gray wolf that no longer exists.

Greyhounds are the fastest dogs in the world. They can run up to 45 miles per hour (72 km/h). Greyhounds could win a long-distance race against cheetahs. Cheetahs can run faster than greyhounds, but greyhounds can run for longer.

Newfoundlands are great lifeguards. Their coats are waterproof. Newfoundlands also have webbed feet. They have thin bits of skin between their toes. This webbing helps Newfoundlands swim faster.

A dog's nose print is as <u>unique</u> as a human fingerprint.

ARE YOU A GENIUS KID?

Now you have lots of fantastic dog facts to amaze your friends and family. But first, let's see what you can remember. It is time to see if you are a genius kid.

Check back through the book if you are not sure.

1. Are dogs omnivores or carnivores?

2. What is the scientific name for domestic dogs?

3. What is a dog's most powerful sense?

Answers:
1. Omnivores, 2. Canis lupus familiaris, 3. Smell.

GLOSSARY

ancestors people or animals in a family who lived a long time ago

breeds a group of the same animals that have similar characteristics

domestic to do with an animal that is tame and often kept by humans

family a way of grouping animals with very similar traits

hibernate a way some animals rest to save energy in the winter

instincts natural patterns of behaviors in animals

muscles the parts of the body that allow the body to move around

unique one of a kind or very rare

weaned getting used to eating things other than their mother's milk

INDEX

canines 5–8

coats 9, 11, 21

ears 8, 16–17

mothers 18–19

packs 15

paws 10, 17

puppies 18–19

tails 11, 17

teeth 9, 16

wolves 4–6, 8, 14–15, 20